Calling Devotional

Praying for Daily Faithfulness

David H. Kim

ISBN-13: 978-1517652623
ISBN-10: 1517652626

To the staff of the Center for Faith & Work.

Your daily faithfulness makes work a joy.

TABLE OF CONTENTS

INTRODUCTION

For some, the idea of discerning one's call is synonymous with finding the right job, but the Biblical notion of calling is much grander. God's calling engages the whole of our lives and was never meant to be isolated to one small aspect of it. When we open ourselves up to God's lead, we can't simply pick and choose which elements we follow and which we ignore. For this reason, the Christian notion of calling must begin first and foremost with the Caller. Discerning our call does not start with self-oriented soul-searching, but with an open and attuned ear towards the Shepherd who guides His sheep (John 10:13-16).

In the gospel, we have the promise that our Great Shepherd leads us and that He is with us both by still waters and in dark valleys (cf. Psalm 23). The question is, will we allow His voice to speak into every aspect of our lives? The answer to this question is encapsulated by what we experience every day. Are we even aware of His presence throughout each day? Do we strive to be faithful to God in the *small* things *each* day? Do we allow His word to guide our motivations, our actions, and our speech? Does the gospel rightly motivate us out of love and gratitude for what Christ has completely accomplished on our behalf?

The goal of this devotional is to help us recognize how God is involved in our daily lives by seeking His guidance through meditation on His Word and reflection upon the past day. This 20-day devotion will guide you through four weeks (weekdays only) of passages of Scripture that deal with stories of how God called people in the Bible. You will hopefully notice some themes as you read through each of these passages. Each devotional has 5 steps and takes 22 minutes. Use a timer to allow yourself to be present for each moment.

My hope is that you will experience in unexpected ways how present God is in our lives and how His grace is at work in us to lead us to greater faithfulness each day. We can never take for granted His guidance as it comes only through the work of Christ. Each time we sense His loving guidance, our only response can be one of gratitude and love towards our Triune God, giving Him the praise and glory that He rightly deserves.

- Rev. David H. Kim, NYC

DAY 1: THE CALL OF ABRAM

1. BEGIN WITH OF AN OPENING PRAYER OF INVITATION (2 MINS)

- Sit comfortably in stillness for these minutes being reminded of God's presence. ☒

- Be reminded that our God brings structure out of the chaos of our days, and leads us with His gracious hand.

- Invite the Holy Spirit who searches our hearts to guide you through this time.

2. AS YOU READ THE BIBLICAL PASSAGE, CONSIDER AND ANSWER THESE TWO QUESTIONS (8 MINS)

A. Identify one thing that this passage reveals about God?

_____

_____

_____

_____

_____

_____

_____

B. Identify one thing that this passage reveals about you/people?

_____

_____

_____

_____

_____

_____

_____

_____

Genesis 12:1–19

The Call of Abram

Now the Lord said to Abram, "Go from your country and your kindred and your father's house to the land that I will show you. ² And I will make of you a great nation, and I will bless you and make your name great,⊠so that you will be a blessing. ³ I will bless those who bless you, and him who dishonors you I will curse, and in you all the families of the earth shall be blessed."

⁴ So Abram went, as the Lord had told him, and Lot went with him. Abram was seventy-five years old when he departed from Haran.⊠⁵ And Abram took Sarai his wife, and Lot his brother's son, and all their possessions that they had gathered, and the people that they had acquired in Haran, and they set out to go to the land of Canaan. When they came to the land of Canaan, ⁶ Abram passed through the land to the place at Shechem, to the oak of Moreh. At that time the Canaanites were in the land. ⁷ Then the Lord appeared to Abram and said, "To your offspring I will give this land." So he built there an altar to the Lord, who had appeared to him. ⁸ From there he moved to the hill country⊠on the east of Bethel and pitched his tent, with Bethel on the west and Ai on the east. And there he built an altar to the Lord and called upon the name of the Lord. ⁹ And Abram journeyed on, still going toward the Negeb.

Abram and Sarai in Egypt

¹⁰ Now there was a famine in the land. So Abram went down to Egypt to sojourn there, for the famine was severe in the land. ¹¹ When he was about to enter Egypt, he said to Sarai his wife, "I know that⊠you are a woman beautiful in appearance, ¹² and when the Egyptians see you, they will say, 'This is his wife.' Then they will kill me, but they will let you live. ¹³ Say you are my sister, that it may go well with me because of you, and that my life may be spared for your sake." ¹⁴ When Abram entered Egypt, the Egyptians saw that the woman was very beautiful. ¹⁵ And when the princes of Pharaoh saw her, they praised her to Pharaoh. And the woman was taken into Pharaoh's house. ¹⁶ And⊠for her sake he dealt well with Abram; and he had sheep, oxen, male donkeys, male servants, female servants, female donkeys, and camels. ¹⁷ But the Lord afflicted Pharaoh and his house with great plagues because of Sarai, Abram's wife. ¹⁸ So Pharaoh called Abram and said, "What is this you have done to me? Why did you not tell me that she was your wife? ¹⁹ Why did you say, 'She is my

sister,' so that I took her for my wife? Now then, here is your wife; take her, and go."

3. REVIEW THE PAST DAY'S EVENTS (3 MINS)

- Remembering that each day is a gift from the Lord, review your day and write down a basic chronology of what happened. ☒

- Does any particular event, meeting, or place stand out to you? ☒In the rush of our days, it is easy to overlook so much. Think about the things you ate, saw, smelled and heard. Remember that God is even in these details.

_____

_____

_____

_____

_____

_____

_____

_____

_____

_____

_____

_____

_____

_____

_____

_____

_____

_____

_____

_____

_____

4. HOW IS GOD CALLING YOU TO GREATER FAITHFULNESS (4 MINS)

- Faithfulness towards God happens in the details of our lives as much as the big decisions we make. He who is faithful with little will be faithful with much.☒

- As you consider the past day, choose one aspect that you feel God is calling you towards greater faithfulness.☒

- How is Christ calling you to change your motivations, your actions and your speech?

_____

_____

_____

_____

_____

_____

_____

_____

_____

_____

5. PRAY FOR THE CHANGE THAT YOU'VE IDENTIFIED (5 MINS)

- Take time to pray for insight in this one particular area of growth. Pray that God would guide you in this change towards greater faithfulness. Pray for the people involved in this matter.☒

- Praise God for His character and His promises and how He is at work in you.

- Consider the gospel and God's immense love towards you to motivate your change towards greater faithfulness.

- Remember that God patiently leads us each day. Our mistakes are redeemable and today's victories do not guarantee success tomorrow.

- Ask that you would be more aware of God's guiding presence in the day to come, and that the lessons learned today would be lived out tomorrow.

DAY 2: THE CALL OF MOSES

1. BEGIN WITH OF AN OPENING PRAYER OF INVITATION (2 MINS)

- Sit comfortably in stillness for these minutes being reminded of God's presence. ☒

- Be reminded that our God brings structure out of the chaos of our days, and leads us with His gracious hand.

- Invite the Holy Spirit who searches our hearts to guide you through this time.

2. AS YOU READ THE BIBLICAL PASSAGE, CONSIDER AND ANSWER THESE TWO QUESTIONS (8 MINS)

A. Identify one thing that this passage reveals about God?

_____

_____

_____

_____

_____

_____

B. Identify one thing that this passage reveals about you/people?

_____

_____

_____

_____

_____

_____

_____

Exodus 3:1–15

The Burning Bush

Now Moses was keeping the flock of his father-in-law, Jethro, the priest of Midian, and he led his flock to the west side of the wilderness and came to Horeb, the mountain of God. ² And the angel of the LORD appeared to him in a flame of fire out of the midst of a bush. He looked, and behold, the bush was burning, yet it was not consumed. ³ And Moses said, "I will turn aside to see this great sight, why the bush is not burned." ⁴ When the LORD saw that he turned aside to see, God called to him out of the bush, "Moses, Moses!" And he said, "Here I am." ⁵ Then he said, "Do not come near; take your sandals off your feet, for the place on which you are standing is holy ground." ⁶ And he said, "I am the God of your father, the God of Abraham, the God of Isaac, and the God of Jacob." And Moses hid his face, for he was afraid to look at God.

⁷ Then the LORD said, "I have surely seen the affliction of my people who are in Egypt and have heard their cry because of their taskmasters. I know their sufferings, ⁸ and I have come down to deliver them out of the hand of the Egyptians and to bring them up out of that land to a good and broad land, a land flowing with milk and honey, to the place of the Canaanites, the Hittites, the Amorites, the Perizzites, the Hivites, and the Jebusites. ⁹ And now, behold, the cry of the people of Israel has come to me, and I have also seen the oppression with which the Egyptians oppress them. ¹⁰ Come, I will send you to Pharaoh that you may bring my people, the children of Israel, out of Egypt." ¹¹ But Moses said to God, "Who am I that I should go to Pharaoh and bring the children of Israel out of Egypt?" ¹² He said, "But I will be with you, and this shall be the sign for you, that I have sent you: when you have brought the people out of Egypt, you shall serve God on this mountain."

¹³ Then Moses said to God, "If I come to the people of Israel and say to them, 'The God of your fathers has sent me to you,' and they ask me, 'What is his name?' what shall I say to them?" ¹⁴ God said to Moses, "I AM WHO I AM." And he said, "Say this to the people of Israel, 'I AM has sent me to you.' " ¹⁵ God also said to Moses, "Say this to the people of Israel, 'The LORD, the God of your fathers, the God of Abraham, the God of Isaac, and the God of Jacob, has sent me to you.' This is my name forever, and thus I am to be remembered throughout all generations.

3. REVIEW THE PAST DAY'S EVENTS (3 MINS)

- Remembering that each day is a gift from the Lord, review your day and write down a basic chronology of what happened. ☒

- Does any particular event, meeting, or place stand out to you? ☒ In the rush of our days, it is easy to overlook so much. Think about the things you ate, saw, smelled and heard. Remember that God is even in these details.

_____

_____

_____

_____

_____

_____

_____

_____

_____

_____

_____

_____

_____

_____

_____

_____

_____

_____

_____

_____

_____

_____

_____

_____

_____

_____

4. HOW IS GOD CALLING YOU TO GREATER FAITHFULNESS (4 MINS)

- Faithfulness towards God happens in the details of our lives as much as the big decisions we make. He who is faithful with little will be faithful with much. ☒

- As you consider the past day, choose one aspect that you feel God is calling you towards greater faithfulness.

- How is Christ calling you to change your motivations, your actions and your speech?

_____

_____

_____

_____

_____

_____

_____

_____

_____

_____

5. PRAY FOR THE CHANGE THAT YOU'VE IDENTIFIED (5 MINS)

- Take time to pray for insight in this one particular area of growth. Pray that God would guide you in this change towards greater faithfulness. Pray for the people involved in this matter. ☒

- Praise God for His character and His promises and how He is at work in you.

- Consider the gospel and God's immense love towards you to motivate your change towards greater faithfulness.

- Remember that God patiently leads us each day. Our mistakes are redeemable and today's victories do not guarantee success tomorrow.

- Ask that you would be more aware of God's guiding presence in the day to come, and that the lessons learned today would be lived out tomorrow.

DAY 3: THE CALL OF MOSES, PT 2

1. BEGIN WITH OF AN OPENING PRAYER OF INVITATION (2 MINS)

- Sit comfortably in stillness for these minutes being reminded of God's presence. ☒

- Be reminded that our God brings structure out of the chaos of our days, and leads us with His gracious hand.

- Invite the Holy Spirit who searches our hearts to guide you through this time.

2. AS YOU READ THE BIBLICAL PASSAGE, CONSIDER AND ANSWER THESE TWO QUESTIONS (8 MINS)

A. Identify one thing that this passage reveals about God?

_____

_____

_____

_____

_____

_____

B. Identify one thing that this passage reveals about you/people?

_____

_____

_____

_____

_____

_____

_____

Exodus 4:10–17

[10] But Moses said to the LORD, "Oh, my Lord, I am not eloquent, either in the past or since you have spoken to your servant, but I am slow of speech and of tongue." [11] Then the LORD said to him, "Who has made man's mouth? Who makes him mute, or deaf, or seeing, or blind? Is it not I, the LORD? [12] Now therefore go, and I will be with your mouth and teach you what you shall speak." [13] But he said, "Oh, my Lord, please send someone else." [14] Then the anger of the LORD was kindled against Moses and he said, "Is there not Aaron, your brother, the Levite? I know that he can speak well. Behold, he is coming out to meet you, and when he sees you, he will be glad in his heart. [15] You shall speak to him and put the words in his mouth, and I will be with your mouth and with his mouth and will teach you both what to do. [16] He shall speak for you to the people, and he shall be your mouth, and you shall be as God to him. [17] And take in your hand this staff, with which you shall do the signs."

3. REVIEW THE PAST DAY'S EVENTS (3 MINS)

- Remembering that each day is a gift from the Lord, review your day and write down a basic chronology of what happened. ☒

- Does any particular event, meeting, or place stand out to you? ☒In the rush of our days, it is easy to overlook so much. Think about the things you ate, saw, smelled and heard. Remember that God is even in these details.

_____

_____

_____

_____

_____

_____

4. HOW IS GOD CALLING YOU TO GREATER FAITHFULNESS (4 MINS)

- Faithfulness towards God happens in the details of our lives as much as the big decisions we make. He who is faithful with little will be faithful with much. ☒

- As you consider the past day, choose one aspect that you feel God is calling you towards greater faithfulness.

- How is Christ calling you to change your motivations, your actions and your speech?

_____

_____

_____

_____

_____

_____

_____

_____

_____

_____

5. PRAY FOR THE CHANGE THAT YOU'VE IDENTIFIED (5 MINS)

- Take time to pray for insight in this one particular area of growth. Pray that God would guide you in this change towards greater faithfulness. Pray for the people involved in this matter. ☒

- Praise God for His character and His promises and how He is at work in you.

- Consider the gospel and God's immense love towards you to motivate your change towards greater faithfulness.

- Remember that God patiently leads us each day. Our mistakes are redeemable and today's victories do not guarantee success tomorrow.

- Ask that you would be more aware of God's guiding presence in the day to come, and that the lessons learned today would be lived out tomorrow.

DAY 4: THE CALL OF BEZALEL

1. BEGIN WITH OF AN OPENING PRAYER OF INVITATION (2 MINS)

- Sit comfortably in stillness for these minutes being reminded of God's presence.☒

- Be reminded that our God brings structure out of the chaos of our days, and leads us with His gracious hand.

- Invite the Holy Spirit who searches our hearts to guide you through this time.

2. AS YOU READ THE BIBLICAL PASSAGE, CONSIDER AND ANSWER THESE TWO QUESTIONS (8 MINS)

A. Identify one thing that this passage reveals about God?

_____

_____

_____

_____

_____

_____

_____

B. Identify one thing that this passage reveals about you/people?

_____

_____

_____

_____

_____

_____

_____

_____

Exodus 31:1–11

Oholiab and Bezalel

The LORD said to Moses, [2] "See, I have called by name Bezalel the son of Uri, son of Hur, of the tribe of Judah, [3] and I have filled him with the Spirit of God, with ability and intelligence, with knowledge and all craftsmanship, [4] to devise artistic designs, to work in gold, silver, and bronze, [5] in cutting stones for setting, and in carving wood, to work in every craft. [6] And behold, I have appointed with him Oholiab, the son of Ahisamach, of the tribe of Dan. And I have given to all able men ability, that they may make all that I have commanded you: [7] the tent of meeting, and the ark of the testimony, and the mercy seat that is on it, and all the furnishings of the tent, [8] the table and its utensils, and the pure lampstand with all its utensils, and the altar of incense, [9] and the altar of burnt offering with all its utensils, and the basin and its stand, [10] and the finely worked garments, the holy garments for Aaron the priest and the garments of his sons, for their service as priests, [11] and the anointing oil and the fragrant incense for the Holy Place. According to all that I have commanded you, they shall do."

3. REVIEW THE PAST DAY'S EVENTS (3 MINS)

- Remembering that each day is a gift from the Lord, review your day and write down a basic chronology of what happened. ☒

- Does any particular event, meeting, or place stand out to you? ☒ In the rush of our days, it is easy to overlook so much. Think about the things you ate, saw, smelled and heard. Remember that God is even in these details.

4. HOW IS GOD CALLING YOU TO GREATER FAITHFULNESS (4 MINS)

- Faithfulness towards God happens in the details of our lives as much as the big decisions we make. He who is faithful with little will be faithful with much.☒

- As you consider the past day, choose one aspect that you feel God is calling you towards greater faithfulness.

- How is Christ calling you to change your motivations, your actions and your speech?

_____

_____

_____

_____

_____

_____

_____

_____

_____

5. PRAY FOR THE CHANGE THAT YOU'VE IDENTIFIED (5 MINS)

- Take time to pray for insight in this one particular area of growth. Pray that God would guide you in this change towards greater faithfulness. Pray for the people involved in this matter.☒

- Praise God for His character and His promises and how He is at work in you.

- Consider the gospel and God's immense love towards you to motivate your change towards greater faithfulness.

- Remember that God patiently leads us each day. Our mistakes are redeemable and today's victories do not guarantee success tomorrow.

- Ask that you would be more aware of God's guiding presence in the day to come, and that the lessons learned today would be lived out tomorrow.

DAY 5: THE CALL OF DEBORAH

1. BEGIN WITH OF AN OPENING PRAYER OF INVITATION (2 MINS)

- Sit comfortably in stillness for these minutes being reminded of God's presence.☒

- Be reminded that our God brings structure out of the chaos of our days, and leads us with His gracious hand.

- Invite the Holy Spirit who searches our hearts to guide you through this time.

2. AS YOU READ THE BIBLICAL PASSAGE, CONSIDER AND ANSWER THESE TWO QUESTIONS (8 MINS)

A. Identify one thing that this passage reveals about God?

_____

_____

_____

_____

_____

_____

_____

B. Identify one thing that this passage reveals about you/people?

_____

_____

_____

_____

_____

_____

_____

Judges 4:4–10 ☒

⁴ Now Deborah, a prophetess, the wife of Lappidoth, was judging Israel at that time. ⁵ She used to sit under the palm of Deborah between Ramah and Bethel in the hill country of Ephraim, and the people of Israel came up to her for judgment. ⁶ She sent and summoned Barak the son of Abinoam from Kedesh-naphtali and said to him, "Has not the LORD, the God of Israel, commanded you, 'Go, gather your men at Mount Tabor, taking 10,000 from the people of Naphtali and the people of Zebulun. ⁷ And I will draw out Sisera, the general of Jabin's army, to meet you by the river Kishon with his chariots and his troops, and I will give him into your hand'?" ⁸ Barak said to her, "If you will go with me, I will go, but if you will not go with me, I will not go." ⁹ And she said, "I will surely go with you. Nevertheless, the road on which you are going will not lead to your glory, for the LORD will sell Sisera into the hand of a woman." Then Deborah arose and went with Barak to Kedesh. ¹⁰ And Barak called out Zebulun and Naphtali to Kedesh. And 10,000 men went up at his heels, and Deborah went up with him.

3. REVIEW THE PAST DAY'S EVENTS (3 MINS)

- Remembering that each day is a gift from the Lord, review your day and write down a basic chronology of what happened. ☒

- Does any particular event, meeting, or place stand out to you? ☒ In the rush of our days, it is easy to overlook so much. Think about the things you ate, saw, smelled and heard. Remember that God is even in these details.

_____

_____

_____

_____

_____

_____

_____

_____

_____

_____

_____

_____

_____

_____

_____

_____

_____

_____

_____

_____

_____

_____

_____

4. HOW IS GOD CALLING YOU TO GREATER FAITHFULNESS (4 MINS)

- Faithfulness towards God happens in the details of our lives as much as the big decisions we make. He who is faithful with little will be faithful with much.☒

- As you consider the past day, choose one aspect that you feel God is calling you towards greater faithfulness.

- How is Christ calling you to change your motivations, your actions and your speech?

_____

_____

_____

_____

_____

_____

_____

_____

_____

5. PRAY FOR THE CHANGE THAT YOU'VE IDENTIFIED (5 MINS)

- Take time to pray for insight in this one particular area of growth. Pray that God would guide you in this change towards greater faithfulness. Pray for the people involved in this matter.☒

- Praise God for His character and His promises and how He is at work in you.

- Consider the gospel and God's immense love towards you to motivate your change towards greater faithfulness.

- Remember that God patiently leads us each day. Our mistakes are redeemable and today's victories do not guarantee success tomorrow.

- Ask that you would be more aware of God's guiding presence in the day to come, and that the lessons learned today would be lived out tomorrow.

DAY 6: THE CALL OF DAVID

1. BEGIN WITH OF AN OPENING PRAYER OF INVITATION (2 MINS)

- Sit comfortably in stillness for these minutes being reminded of God's presence.☒

- Be reminded that our God brings structure out of the chaos of our days, and leads us with His gracious hand.

- Invite the Holy Spirit who searches our hearts to guide you through this time.

2. AS YOU READ THE BIBLICAL PASSAGE, CONSIDER AND ANSWER THESE TWO QUESTIONS (8 MINS)

A. Identify one thing that this passage reveals about God?

_____

_____

_____

_____

_____

_____

B. Identify one thing that this passage reveals about you/people?

_____

_____

_____

_____

_____

_____

_____

_____

1 Samuel 16:1–13

David Anointed King

The LORD said to Samuel, "How long will you grieve over Saul, since I have rejected him from being king over Israel? Fill your horn with oil, and go. I will send you to Jesse the Bethlehemite, for I have provided for myself a king among his sons." ² And Samuel said, "How can I go? If Saul hears it, he will kill me." And the LORD said, "Take a heifer with you and say, 'I have come to sacrifice to the LORD.' ³ And invite Jesse to the sacrifice, and I will show you what you shall do. And you shall anoint for me him whom I declare to you." ⁴ Samuel did what the LORD commanded and came to Bethlehem. The elders of the city came to meet him trembling and said, "Do you come peaceably?" ⁵ And he said, "Peaceably; I have come to sacrifice to the LORD. Consecrate yourselves, and come with me to the sacrifice." And he consecrated Jesse and his sons and invited them to the sacrifice.

⁶ When they came, he looked on Eliab and thought, "Surely the LORD's anointed is before him." ⁷ But the LORD said to Samuel, "Do not look on his appearance or on the height of his stature, because I have rejected him. For the LORD sees not as man sees: man looks on the outward appearance, but the LORD looks on the heart." ⁸ Then Jesse called Abinadab and made him pass before Samuel. And he said, "Neither has the LORD chosen this one." ⁹ Then Jesse made Shammah pass by. And he said, "Neither has the LORD chosen this one." ¹⁰ And Jesse made seven of his sons pass before Samuel. And Samuel said to Jesse, "The LORD has not chosen these." ¹¹ Then Samuel said to Jesse, "Are all your sons here?" And he said, "There remains yet the youngest, but behold, he is keeping the sheep." And Samuel said to Jesse, "Send and get him, for we will not sit down till he comes here." ¹² And he sent and brought him in. Now he was ruddy and had beautiful eyes and was handsome. And the LORD said, "Arise, anoint him, for this is he." ¹³ Then Samuel took the horn of oil and anointed him in the midst of his brothers. And the Spirit of the LORD rushed upon David from that day forward. And Samuel rose up and went to Ramah.

3. REVIEW THE PAST DAY'S EVENTS (3 MINS)

- Remembering that each day is a gift from the Lord, review your day and write down a basic chronology of what happened. ☒

- Does any particular event, meeting, or place stand out to you? ☒In the rush of our days, it is easy to overlook so much. Think about the things you ate, saw, smelled and heard. Remember that God is even in these details.

_____

_____

_____

_____

_____

_____

_____

_____

_____

_____

_____

_____

_____

_____

_____

_____

_____

_____

_____

_____

_____

_____

_____

4. HOW IS GOD CALLING YOU TO GREATER FAITHFULNESS (4 MINS)

- Faithfulness towards God happens in the details of our lives as much as the big decisions we make. He who is faithful with little will be faithful with much.☒

- As you consider the past day, choose one aspect that you feel God is calling you towards greater faithfulness.

- How is Christ calling you to change your motivations, your actions and your speech?

_____

_____

_____

_____

_____

_____

_____

_____

_____

_____

5. PRAY FOR THE CHANGE THAT YOU'VE IDENTIFIED (5 MINS)

- Take time to pray for insight in this one particular area of growth. Pray that God would guide you in this change towards greater faithfulness. Pray for the people involved in this matter.☒

- Praise God for His character and His promises and how He is at work in you.

- Consider the gospel and God's immense love towards you to motivate your change towards greater faithfulness.

- Remember that God patiently leads us each day. Our mistakes are redeemable and today's victories do not guarantee success tomorrow.

- Ask that you would be more aware of God's guiding presence in the day to come, and that the lessons learned today would be lived out tomorrow.

DAY 7: THE CALL OF ISAIAH

1. BEGIN WITH OF AN OPENING PRAYER OF INVITATION (2 MINS)

- Sit comfortably in stillness for these minutes being reminded of God's presence.☒

- Be reminded that our God brings structure out of the chaos of our days, and leads us with His gracious hand.

- Invite the Holy Spirit who searches our hearts to guide you through this time.

2. AS YOU READ THE BIBLICAL PASSAGE, CONSIDER AND ANSWER THESE TWO QUESTIONS (8 MINS)

A. Identify one thing that this passage reveals about God?

_____

_____

_____

_____

_____

_____

_____

_____

B. Identify one thing that this passage reveals about you/people?

_____

_____

_____

_____

_____

_____

_____

Isaiah 6:1–13

Isaiah's Vision of the Lord

In the year that King Uzziah died I saw the Lord sitting upon a throne, high and lifted up; and the train of his robe filled the temple. ² Above him stood the seraphim. Each had six wings: with two he covered his face, and with two he covered his feet, and with two he flew. ³ And one called to another and said:

> "Holy, holy, holy is the LORD of hosts;
> the whole earth is full of his glory!"

⁴ And the foundations of the thresholds shook at the voice of him who called, and the house was filled with smoke. ⁵ And I said: "Woe is me! For I am lost; for I am a man of unclean lips, and I dwell in the midst of a people of unclean lips; for my eyes have seen the King, the LORD of hosts!"

⁶ Then one of the seraphim flew to me, having in his hand a burning coal that he had taken with tongs from the altar. ⁷ And he touched my mouth and said: "Behold, this has touched your lips; your guilt is taken away, and your sin atoned for."

Isaiah's Commission from the Lord

⁸ And I heard the voice of the Lord saying, "Whom shall I send, and who will go for us?" Then I said, "Here I am! Send me." ⁹ And he said, "Go, and say to this people:

> " 'Keep on hearing, but do not understand;
> keep on seeing, but do not perceive.'

> 10   Make the heart of this people dull,
> and their ears heavy, and blind their eyes;
> lest they see with their eyes, and hear with their ears,
> and understand with their hearts, and turn and be healed."
> 11   Then I said, "How long, O Lord?"
> And he said: "Until cities lie waste without inhabitant,
> and houses without people, and the land is a desolate waste,
> 12   and the Lord removes people far away,
> and the forsaken places are many in the midst of the land.
> 13   And though a tenth remain in it, it will be burned again,
> like a terebinth or an oak,
> whose stump remains when it is felled."
> The holy seed is its stump.

3. REVIEW THE PAST DAY'S EVENTS (3 MINS)

- Remembering that each day is a gift from the Lord, review your day and write down a basic chronology of what happened. ☒

- Does any particular event, meeting, or place stand out to you? ☒ In the rush of our days, it is easy to overlook so much. Think about the things you ate, saw, smelled and heard. Remember that God is even in these details.

4. HOW IS GOD CALLING YOU TO GREATER FAITHFULNESS (4 MINS)

- Faithfulness towards God happens in the details of our lives as much as the big decisions we make. He who is faithful with little will be faithful with much.☒

- As you consider the past day, choose one aspect that you feel God is calling you towards greater faithfulness.

- How is Christ calling you to change your motivations, your actions and your speech?

_____

_____

_____

_____

_____

_____

_____

_____

_____

5. PRAY FOR THE CHANGE THAT YOU'VE IDENTIFIED (5 MINS)

- Take time to pray for insight in this one particular area of growth. Pray that God would guide you in this change towards greater faithfulness. Pray for the people involved in this matter.☒

- Praise God for His character and His promises and how He is at work in you.

- Consider the gospel and God's immense love towards you to motivate your change towards greater faithfulness.

- Remember that God patiently leads us each day. Our mistakes are redeemable and today's victories do not guarantee success tomorrow.

- Ask that you would be more aware of God's guiding presence in the day to come, and that the lessons learned today would be lived out tomorrow.

DAY 8: THE CALL OF JEREMIAH

1. BEGIN WITH OF AN OPENING PRAYER OF INVITATION (2 MINS)

- Sit comfortably in stillness for these minutes being reminded of God's presence.☒

- Be reminded that our God brings structure out of the chaos of our days, and leads us with His gracious hand.

- Invite the Holy Spirit who searches our hearts to guide you through this time.

2. AS YOU READ THE BIBLICAL PASSAGE, CONSIDER AND ANSWER THESE TWO QUESTIONS (8 MINS)

A. Identify one thing that this passage reveals about God?

_____

_____

_____

_____

_____

_____

B. Identify one thing that this passage reveals about you/people?

_____

_____

_____

_____

_____

_____

_____

_____

Jeremiah 1:4–10, 20:7–9

The Call of Jeremiah

⁴ Now the word of the LORD came to me, saying,

> 5   "Before I formed you in the womb I knew you,
> and before you were born I consecrated you;
> I appointed you a prophet to the nations."

⁶ Then I said, "Ah, Lord GOD! Behold, I do not know how to speak, for I am only a youth." ⁷ But the LORD said to me,

> "Do not say, 'I am only a youth';
> for to all to whom I send you, you shall go,
> and whatever I command you, you shall speak.
> 8   Do not be afraid of them,
> for I am with you to deliver you,

declares the LORD."

⁹ Then the LORD put out his hand and touched my mouth. And the LORD said to me,

> "Behold, I have put my words in your mouth.
> 10   See, I have set you this day over nations and over kingdoms,
> to pluck up and to break down,
> to destroy and to overthrow,
> to build and to plant."

Jeremiah 20:7–9 (ESV)

> 7   O LORD, you have deceived me, and I was deceived;
> you are stronger than I, and you have prevailed.
> I have become a laughingstock all the day;

everyone mocks me.

> 8   For whenever I speak, I cry out,

I shout, "Violence and destruction!"

> For the word of the LORD has become for me

a reproach and derision all day long.

> 9   If I say, "I will not mention him,

or speak any more in his name,"

> there is in my heart as it were a burning fire

shut up in my bones,

> and I am weary with holding it in, and I cannot.

3. REVIEW THE PAST DAY'S EVENTS (3 MINS)

- Remembering that each day is a gift from the Lord, review your day and write down a basic chronology of what happened. ☒

- Does any particular event, meeting, or place stand out to you? ☒In the rush of our days, it is easy to overlook so much. Think about the things you ate, saw, smelled and heard. Remember that God is even in these details.

4. HOW IS GOD CALLING YOU TO GREATER FAITHFULNESS (4 MINS)

- Faithfulness towards God happens in the details of our lives as much as the big decisions we make. He who is faithful with little will be faithful with much.☒

- As you consider the past day, choose one aspect that you feel God is calling you towards greater faithfulness.

- How is Christ calling you to change your motivations, your actions and your speech?

_____

_____

_____

_____

_____

_____

_____

_____

_____

_____

5. PRAY FOR THE CHANGE THAT YOU'VE IDENTIFIED (5 MINS)

- Take time to pray for insight in this one particular area of growth. Pray that God would guide you in this change towards greater faithfulness. Pray for the people involved in this matter.☒

- Praise God for His character and His promises and how He is at work in you.

- Consider the gospel and God's immense love towards you to motivate your change towards greater faithfulness.

- Remember that God patiently leads us each day. Our mistakes are redeemable and today's victories do not guarantee success tomorrow.

- Ask that you would be more aware of God's guiding presence in the day to come, and that the lessons learned today would be lived out tomorrow.

DAY 9: THE CALL OF MARY

1. BEGIN WITH OF AN OPENING PRAYER OF INVITATION (2 MINS)

- Sit comfortably in stillness for these minutes being reminded of God's presence.☒

- Be reminded that our God brings structure out of the chaos of our days, and leads us with His gracious hand.

- Invite the Holy Spirit who searches our hearts to guide you through this time.

2. AS YOU READ THE BIBLICAL PASSAGE, CONSIDER AND ANSWER THESE TWO QUESTIONS (8 MINS)

A. Identify one thing that this passage reveals about God?

_____

_____

_____

_____

_____

_____

_____

_____

B. Identify one thing that this passage reveals about you/people?

_____

_____

_____

_____

_____

_____

Luke 1:26–56

Birth of Jesus Foretold

26 In the sixth month the angel Gabriel was sent from God to a city of Galilee named Nazareth, 27 to a virgin betrothed to a man whose name was Joseph, of the house of David. And the virgin's name was Mary. 28 And he came to her and said, "Greetings, O favored one, the Lord is with you!" 29 But she was greatly troubled at the saying, and tried to discern what sort of greeting this might be. 30 And the angel said to her, "Do not be afraid, Mary, for you have found favor with God. 31 And behold, you will conceive in your womb and bear a son, and you shall call his name Jesus. 32 He will be great and will be called the Son of the Most High. And the Lord God will give to him the throne of his father David, 33 and he will reign over the house of Jacob forever, and of his kingdom there will be no end."

34 And Mary said to the angel, "How will this be, since I am a virgin?"

35 And the angel answered her, "The Holy Spirit will come upon you, and the power of the Most High will overshadow you; therefore the child to be born will be called holy—the Son of God. 36 And behold, your relative Elizabeth in her old age has also conceived a son, and this is the sixth month with her who was called barren. 37 For nothing will be impossible with God." 38 And Mary said, "Behold, I am the servant of the Lord; let it be to me according to your word." And the angel departed from her.

Mary Visits Elizabeth

39 In those days Mary arose and went with haste into the hill country, to a town in Judah, 40 and she entered the house of Zechariah and greeted Elizabeth. 41 And when Elizabeth heard the greeting of Mary, the baby leaped in her womb. And Elizabeth was filled with the Holy Spirit, 42 and she exclaimed with a loud cry, "Blessed are you among women, and blessed is the fruit of your womb! 43 And why is this granted to me that the mother of my Lord should come to me? 44 For behold, when the sound of your greeting came to my ears, the baby in my womb leaped for joy. 45 And blessed is she who believed that there would be a fulfillment of what was spoken to her from the Lord."

Mary's Song of Praise: The Magnificat

⁴⁶ And Mary said,

      "My soul magnifies the Lord,
⁴⁷   and my spirit rejoices in God my Savior,
⁴⁸   for he has looked on the humble estate of his servant.
For behold, from now on all generations will call me blessed;
⁴⁹   for he who is mighty has done great things for me,
and holy is his name.
⁵⁰   And his mercy is for those who fear him
from generation to generation.
⁵¹   He has shown strength with his arm;
he has scattered the proud in the thoughts of their hearts;
⁵²   he has brought down the mighty from their thrones
and exalted those of humble estate;
⁵³   he has filled the hungry with good things,
and the rich he has sent away empty.
⁵⁴   He has helped his servant Israel,
in remembrance of his mercy,
⁵⁵   as he spoke to our fathers,
to Abraham and to his offspring forever."

⁵⁶ And Mary remained with her about three months and returned to her home.

3. REVIEW THE PAST DAY'S EVENTS (3 MINS)

- Remembering that each day is a gift from the Lord, review your day and write down a basic chronology of what happened. ☒

- Does any particular event, meeting, or place stand out to you? ☒In the rush of our days, it is easy to overlook so much. Think about the things you ate, saw, smelled and heard. Remember that God is even in these details.

_____

_____

_____

_____

_____

_____

_____

4. HOW IS GOD CALLING YOU TO GREATER FAITHFULNESS (4 MINS)

- Faithfulness towards God happens in the details of our lives as much as the big decisions we make. He who is faithful with little will be faithful with much. ☒

- As you consider the past day, choose one aspect that you feel God is calling you towards greater faithfulness.

- How is Christ calling you to change your motivations, your actions and your speech?

_____

_____

_____

_____

_____

_____

_____

_____

_____

_____

5. PRAY FOR THE CHANGE THAT YOU'VE IDENTIFIED (5 MINS)

- Take time to pray for insight in this one particular area of growth. Pray that God would guide you in this change towards greater faithfulness. Pray for the people involved in this matter. ☒

- Praise God for His character and His promises and how He is at work in you.

- Consider the gospel and God's immense love towards you to motivate your change towards greater faithfulness.

- Remember that God patiently leads us each day. Our mistakes are redeemable and today's victories do not guarantee success tomorrow.

- Ask that you would be more aware of God's guiding presence in the day to come, and that the lessons learned today would be lived out tomorrow.

DAY 10: THE CALL OF THE DISCIPLES

1. BEGIN WITH OF AN OPENING PRAYER OF INVITATION (2 MINS)

- Sit comfortably in stillness for these minutes being reminded of God's presence. ☒

- Be reminded that our God brings structure out of the chaos of our days, and leads us with His gracious hand.

- Invite the Holy Spirit who searches our hearts to guide you through this time.

2. AS YOU READ THE BIBLICAL PASSAGE, CONSIDER AND ANSWER THESE TWO QUESTIONS (8 MINS)

A. Identify one thing that this passage reveals about God?

_____

_____

_____

_____

_____

_____

B. Identify one thing that this passage reveals about you/people?

_____

_____

_____

_____

_____

_____

_____

_____

Matthew 4:18–22

Jesus Calls the First Disciples

[18] While walking by the Sea of Galilee, he saw two brothers, Simon (who is called Peter) and Andrew his brother, casting a net into the sea, for they were fishermen. [19] And he said to them, "Follow me, and I will make you fishers of men." [20] Immediately they left their nets and followed him. [21] And going on from there he saw two other brothers, James the son of Zebedee and John his brother, in the boat with Zebedee their father, mending their nets, and he called them. [22] Immediately they left the boat and their father and followed him.

3. REVIEW THE PAST DAY'S EVENTS (3 MINS)

- Remembering that each day is a gift from the Lord, review your day and write down a basic chronology of what happened. ☒

- Does any particular event, meeting, or place stand out to you? ☒ In the rush of our days, it is easy to overlook so much. Think about the things you ate, saw, smelled and heard. Remember that God is even in these details.

_____

_____

_____

_____

_____

_____

_____

_____

_____

_____

_____

_____

_____

_____

_____

_____

_____

_____

_____

_____

_____

_____

_____

4. HOW IS GOD CALLING YOU TO GREATER FAITHFULNESS (4 MINS)

- Faithfulness towards God happens in the details of our lives as much as the big decisions we make. He who is faithful with little will be faithful with much.☒

- As you consider the past day, choose one aspect that you feel God is calling you towards greater faithfulness.

- How is Christ calling you to change your motivations, your actions and your speech?

_____

_____

_____

_____

_____

_____

_____

_____

_____

5. PRAY FOR THE CHANGE THAT YOU'VE IDENTIFIED (5 MINS)

- Take time to pray for insight in this one particular area of growth. Pray that God would guide you in this change towards greater faithfulness. Pray for the people involved in this matter.☒

- Praise God for His character and His promises and how He is at work in you.

- Consider the gospel and God's immense love towards you to motivate your change towards greater faithfulness.

- Remember that God patiently leads us each day. Our mistakes are redeemable and today's victories do not guarantee success tomorrow.

- Ask that you would be more aware of God's guiding presence in the day to come, and that the lessons learned today would be lived out tomorrow.

DAY 11: THE CALL OF NICODEMUS

1. BEGIN WITH OF AN OPENING PRAYER OF INVITATION (2 MINS)

- Sit comfortably in stillness for these minutes being reminded of God's presence.☒

- Be reminded that our God brings structure out of the chaos of our days, and leads us with His gracious hand.

- Invite the Holy Spirit who searches our hearts to guide you through this time.

2. AS YOU READ THE BIBLICAL PASSAGE, CONSIDER AND ANSWER THESE TWO QUESTIONS (8 MINS)

A. Identify one thing that this passage reveals about God?

_____

_____

_____

_____

_____

_____

_____

B. Identify one thing that this passage reveals about you/people?

_____

_____

_____

_____

_____

_____

_____

_____

John 3:1–21

You Must Be Born Again

Now there was a man of the Pharisees named Nicodemus, a ruler of the Jews. ² This man came to Jesus by night and said to him, "Rabbi, we know that you are a teacher come from God, for no one can do these signs that you do unless God is with him." ³ Jesus answered him, "Truly, truly, I say to you, unless one is born again he cannot see the kingdom of God." ⁴ Nicodemus said to him, "How can a man be born when he is old? Can he enter a second time into his mother's womb and be born?" ⁵ Jesus answered, "Truly, truly, I say to you, unless one is born of water and the Spirit, he cannot enter the kingdom of God. ⁶ That which is born of the flesh is flesh, and that which is born of the Spirit is spirit. ⁷ Do not marvel that I said to you, 'You must be born again.' ⁸ The wind blows where it wishes, and you hear its sound, but you do not know where it comes from or where it goes. So it is with everyone who is born of the Spirit."

⁹ Nicodemus said to him, "How can these things be?" ¹⁰ Jesus answered him, "Are you the teacher of Israel and yet you do not understand these things? ¹¹ Truly, truly, I say to you, we speak of what we know, and bear witness to what we have seen, but you do not receive our testimony. ¹² If I have told you earthly things and you do not believe, how can you believe if I tell you heavenly things? ¹³ No one has ascended into heaven except he who descended from heaven, the Son of Man. ¹⁴ And as Moses lifted up the serpent in the wilderness, so must the Son of Man be lifted up, ¹⁵ that whoever believes in him may have eternal life.

¹⁶ "For God so loved the world, that he gave his only Son, that whoever believes in him should not perish but have eternal life. ¹⁷ For God did not send his Son into the world to condemn the world, but in order that the world might be saved through him. ¹⁸ Whoever believes in him is not condemned, but whoever does not believe is condemned already, because he has not believed in the name of the only Son of God. ¹⁹ And this is the judgment: the light has come into the world, and people loved the darkness rather than the light because their works were evil. ²⁰ For everyone who does wicked things hates the light and does not come to the light, lest his works should be exposed. ²¹ But whoever does what is true comes to the light, so that it may be clearly seen that his works have been carried out in God."

3. REVIEW THE PAST DAY'S EVENTS (3 MINS)

- Remembering that each day is a gift from the Lord, review your day and write down a basic chronology of what happened. ⊠

- Does any particular event, meeting, or place stand out to you? ⊠In the rush of our days, it is easy to overlook so much. Think about the things you ate, saw, smelled and heard. Remember that God is even in these details.

4. HOW IS GOD CALLING YOU TO GREATER FAITHFULNESS (4 MINS)

- Faithfulness towards God happens in the details of our lives as much as the big decisions we make. He who is faithful with little will be faithful with much.☒

- As you consider the past day, choose one aspect that you feel God is calling you towards greater faithfulness.

- How is Christ calling you to change your motivations, your actions and your speech?

_____

_____

_____

_____

_____

_____

_____

_____

_____

_____

_____

5. PRAY FOR THE CHANGE THAT YOU'VE IDENTIFIED (5 MINS)

- Take time to pray for insight in this one particular area of growth. Pray that God would guide you in this change towards greater faithfulness. Pray for the people involved in this matter.☒

- Praise God for His character and His promises and how He is at work in you.

- Consider the gospel and God's immense love towards you to motivate your change towards greater faithfulness.

- Remember that God patiently leads us each day. Our mistakes are redeemable and today's victories do not guarantee success tomorrow.

- Ask that you would be more aware of God's guiding presence in the day to come, and that the lessons learned today would be lived out tomorrow.

DAY 12: THE CALL OF THE ETHIOPIAN

1. BEGIN WITH OF AN OPENING PRAYER OF INVITATION (2 MINS)

- Sit comfortably in stillness for these minutes being reminded of God's presence.☒

- Be reminded that our God brings structure out of the chaos of our days, and leads us with His gracious hand.

- Invite the Holy Spirit who searches our hearts to guide you through this time.

2. AS YOU READ THE BIBLICAL PASSAGE, CONSIDER AND ANSWER THESE TWO QUESTIONS (8 MINS)

A. Identify one thing that this passage reveals about God?

_____

_____

_____

_____

_____

_____

_____

B. Identify one thing that this passage reveals about you/people?

_____

_____

_____

_____

_____

_____

_____

Acts 8:26–38

Philip and the Ethiopian Eunuch

26 Now an angel of the Lord said to Philip, "Rise and go toward the south to the road that goes down from Jerusalem to Gaza." This is a desert place. 27 And he rose and went. And there was an Ethiopian, a eunuch, a court official of Candace, queen of the Ethiopians, who was in charge of all her treasure. He had come to Jerusalem to worship 28 and was returning, seated in his chariot, and he was reading the prophet Isaiah. 29 And the Spirit said to Philip, "Go over and join this chariot." 30 So Philip ran to him and heard him reading Isaiah the prophet and asked, "Do you understand what you are reading?" 31 And he said, "How can I, unless someone guides me?" And he invited Philip to come up and sit with him. 32 Now the passage of the Scripture that he was reading was this:

> "Like a sheep he was led to the slaughter
> and like a lamb before its shearer is silent,
> so he opens not his mouth.
> 33   In his humiliation justice was denied him.
> Who can describe his generation?
> For his life is taken away from the earth."

34 And the eunuch said to Philip, "About whom, I ask you, does the prophet say this, about himself or about someone else?" 35 Then Philip opened his mouth, and beginning with this Scripture he told him the good news about Jesus. 36 And as they were going along the road they came to some water, and the eunuch said, "See, here is water! What prevents me from being baptized?" 38 And he commanded the chariot to stop, and they both went down into the water, Philip and the eunuch, and he baptized him.

3. REVIEW THE PAST DAY'S EVENTS (3 MINS)

- Remembering that each day is a gift from the Lord, review your day and write down a basic chronology of what happened. ☒

- Does any particular event, meeting, or place stand out to you? ☒ In the rush of our days, it is easy to overlook so much. Think about the things you ate, saw, smelled and heard. Remember that God is even in these details.

_____

_____

_____

_____

_____

_____

_____

_____

_____

_____

_____

_____

_____

_____

_____

_____

_____

_____

_____

_____

_____

_____

_____

_____

_____

4. HOW IS GOD CALLING YOU TO GREATER FAITHFULNESS (4 MINS)

- Faithfulness towards God happens in the details of our lives as much as the big decisions we make. He who is faithful with little will be faithful with much.☒

- As you consider the past day, choose one aspect that you feel God is calling you towards greater faithfulness.

- How is Christ calling you to change your motivations, your actions and your speech?

_____

_____

_____

_____

_____

_____

_____

_____

_____

_____

5. PRAY FOR THE CHANGE THAT YOU'VE IDENTIFIED (5 MINS)

- Take time to pray for insight in this one particular area of growth. Pray that God would guide you in this change towards greater faithfulness. Pray for the people involved in this matter.☒

- Praise God for His character and His promises and how He is at work in you.

- Consider the gospel and God's immense love towards you to motivate your change towards greater faithfulness.

- Remember that God patiently leads us each day. Our mistakes are redeemable and today's victories do not guarantee success tomorrow.

- Ask that you would be more aware of God's guiding presence in the day to come, and that the lessons learned today would be lived out tomorrow.

DAY 13: THE CALL OF PAUL

1. BEGIN WITH OF AN OPENING PRAYER OF INVITATION (2 MINS)

- Sit comfortably in stillness for these minutes being reminded of God's presence. ☒

- Be reminded that our God brings structure out of the chaos of our days, and leads us with His gracious hand.

- Invite the Holy Spirit who searches our hearts to guide you through this time.

2. AS YOU READ THE BIBLICAL PASSAGE, CONSIDER AND ANSWER THESE TWO QUESTIONS (8 MINS)

A. Identify one thing that this passage reveals about God?

_____

_____

_____

_____

_____

_____

_____

B. Identify one thing that this passage reveals about you/people?

_____

_____

_____

_____

_____

_____

_____

Acts 9:1–19

The Conversion of Saul

But Saul, still breathing threats and murder against the disciples of the Lord, went to the high priest 2 and asked him for letters to the synagogues at Damascus, so that if he found any belonging to the Way, men or women, he might bring them bound to Jerusalem. 3 Now as he went on his way, he approached Damascus, and suddenly a light from heaven shone around him. 4 And falling to the ground he heard a voice saying to him, "Saul, Saul, why are you persecuting me?" 5 And he said, "Who are you, Lord?" And he said, "I am Jesus, whom you are persecuting. 6 But rise and enter the city, and you will be told what you are to do." 7 The men who were traveling with him stood speechless, hearing the voice but seeing no one. 8 Saul rose from the ground, and although his eyes were opened, he saw nothing. So they led him by the hand and brought him into Damascus. 9 And for three days he was without sight, and neither ate nor drank.

10 Now there was a disciple at Damascus named Ananias. The Lord said to him in a vision, "Ananias." And he said, "Here I am, Lord." 11 And the Lord said to him, "Rise and go to the street called Straight, and at the house of Judas look for a man of Tarsus named Saul, for behold, he is praying, 12 and he has seen in a vision a man named Ananias come in and lay his hands on him so that he might regain his sight." 13 But Ananias answered, "Lord, I have heard from many about this man, how much evil he has done to your saints at Jerusalem. 14 And here he has authority from the chief priests to bind all who call on your name." 15 But the Lord said to him, "Go, for he is a chosen instrument of mine to carry my name before the Gentiles and kings and the children of Israel. 16 For I will show him how much he must suffer for the sake of my name." 17 So Ananias departed and entered the house. And laying his hands on him he said, "Brother Saul, the Lord Jesus who appeared to you on the road by which you came has sent me so that you may regain your sight and be filled with the Holy Spirit." 18 And immediately something like scales fell from his eyes, and he regained his sight. Then he rose and was baptized; 19 and taking food, he was strengthened. For some days he was with the disciples at Damascus.

3. REVIEW THE PAST DAY'S EVENTS (3 MINS)

- Remembering that each day is a gift from the Lord, review your day and write down a basic chronology of what happened. ☒

- Does any particular event, meeting, or place stand out to you? ☒ In the rush of our days, it is easy to overlook so much. Think about the things you ate, saw, smelled and heard. Remember that God is even in these details.

_____

_____

_____

_____

_____

_____

_____

_____

_____

_____

_____

_____

_____

_____

_____

_____

_____

_____

_____

_____

_____

_____

_____

_____

_____

_____

4. HOW IS GOD CALLING YOU TO GREATER FAITHFULNESS (4 MINS)

- Faithfulness towards God happens in the details of our lives as much as the big decisions we make. He who is faithful with little will be faithful with much.☒

- As you consider the past day, choose one aspect that you feel God is calling you towards greater faithfulness.

- How is Christ calling you to change your motivations, your actions and your speech?

_____

_____

_____

_____

_____

_____

_____

_____

_____

5. PRAY FOR THE CHANGE THAT YOU'VE IDENTIFIED (5 MINS)

- Take time to pray for insight in this one particular area of growth. Pray that God would guide you in this change towards greater faithfulness. Pray for the people involved in this matter.☒

- Praise God for His character and His promises and how He is at work in you.

- Consider the gospel and God's immense love towards you to motivate your change towards greater faithfulness.

- Remember that God patiently leads us each day. Our mistakes are redeemable and today's victories do not guarantee success tomorrow.

- Ask that you would be more aware of God's guiding presence in the day to come, and that the lessons learned today would be lived out tomorrow.

DAY 14: THE CALL TO FREEDOM

1. BEGIN WITH OF AN OPENING PRAYER OF INVITATION (2 MINS)

- Sit comfortably in stillness for these minutes being reminded of God's presence.☒

- Be reminded that our God brings structure out of the chaos of our days, and leads us with His gracious hand.

- Invite the Holy Spirit who searches our hearts to guide you through this time.

2. AS YOU READ THE BIBLICAL PASSAGE, CONSIDER AND ANSWER THESE TWO QUESTIONS (8 MINS)

A. Identify one thing that this passage reveals about God?

_____

_____

_____

_____

_____

_____

_____

B. Identify one thing that this passage reveals about you/people?

_____

_____

_____

_____

_____

_____

_____

Galatians 5:1-15

Christ Has Set Us Free

For freedom Christ has set us free; stand firm therefore, and do not submit again to a yoke of slavery.

²Look: I, Paul, say to you that if you accept circumcision, Christ will be of no advantage to you. ³I testify again to every man who accepts circumcision that he is obligated to keep the whole law. ⁴You are severed from Christ, you who would be justified by the law; you have fallen away from grace. ⁵For through the Spirit, by faith, we ourselves eagerly wait for the hope of righteousness. ⁶For in Christ Jesus neither circumcision nor uncircumcision counts for anything, but only faith working through love.

⁷You were running well. Who hindered you from obeying the truth? ⁸This persuasion is not from him who calls you. ⁹A little leaven leavens the whole lump. ¹⁰I have confidence in the Lord that you will take no other view, and the one who is troubling you will bear the penalty, whoever he is. ¹¹But if I, brothers, still preach circumcision, why am I still being persecuted? In that case the offense of the cross has been removed. ¹²I wish those who unsettle you would emasculate themselves!

¹³For you were called to freedom, brothers. Only do not use your freedom as an opportunity for the flesh, but through love serve one another. ¹⁴For the whole law is fulfilled in one word: "You shall love your neighbor as yourself." ¹⁵But if you bite and devour one another, watch out that you are not consumed by one another.

3. REVIEW THE PAST DAY'S EVENTS (3 MINS)

- Remembering that each day is a gift from the Lord, review your day and write down a basic chronology of what happened. ☒

- Does any particular event, meeting, or place stand out to you? ☒In the rush of our days, it is easy to overlook so much. Think about the things you ate, saw, smelled and heard. Remember that God is even in these details.

_____

_____

_____

_____

_____

_____

_____

_____

_____

_____

_____

_____

_____

_____

_____

_____

_____

_____

_____

_____

_____

_____

_____

_____

_____

4. HOW IS GOD CALLING YOU TO GREATER FAITHFULNESS (4 MINS)

- Faithfulness towards God happens in the details of our lives as much as the big decisions we make. He who is faithful with little will be faithful with much. ☒

- As you consider the past day, choose one aspect that you feel God is calling you towards greater faithfulness.

- How is Christ calling you to change your motivations, your actions and your speech?

_____

_____

_____

_____

_____

_____

_____

_____

_____

5. PRAY FOR THE CHANGE THAT YOU'VE IDENTIFIED (5 MINS)

- Take time to pray for insight in this one particular area of growth. Pray that God would guide you in this change towards greater faithfulness. Pray for the people involved in this matter. ☒

- Praise God for His character and His promises and how He is at work in you.

- Consider the gospel and God's immense love towards you to motivate your change towards greater faithfulness.

- Remember that God patiently leads us each day. Our mistakes are redeemable and today's victories do not guarantee success tomorrow.

- Ask that you would be more aware of God's guiding presence in the day to come, and that the lessons learned today would be lived out tomorrow.

DAY 15: THE CALL FOR UNITY

1. BEGIN WITH OF AN OPENING PRAYER OF INVITATION (2 MINS)

- Sit comfortably in stillness for these minutes being reminded of God's presence. ☒

- Be reminded that our God brings structure out of the chaos of our days, and leads us with His gracious hand.

- Invite the Holy Spirit who searches our hearts to guide you through this time.

2. AS YOU READ THE BIBLICAL PASSAGE, CONSIDER AND ANSWER THESE TWO QUESTIONS (8 MINS)

A. Identify one thing that this passage reveals about God?

_____

_____

_____

_____

_____

_____

_____

B. Identify one thing that this passage reveals about you/people?

_____

_____

_____

_____

_____

_____

_____

_____

_____

_____

Ephesians 4:1–16

Unity in the Body of Christ

I therefore, a prisoner for the Lord, urge you to walk in a manner worthy of the calling to which you have been called, ² with all humility and gentleness, with patience, bearing with one another in love, ³ eager to maintain the unity of the Spirit in the bond of peace. ⁴ There is one body and one Spirit—just as you were called to the one hope that belongs to your call— ⁵ one Lord, one faith, one baptism, ⁶ one God and Father of all, who is over all and through all and in all. ⁷ But grace was given to each one of us according to the measure of Christ's gift. ⁸ Therefore it says,

"When he ascended on high he led a host of captives,
and he gave gifts to men."

⁹ (In saying, "He ascended," what does it mean but that he had also descended into the lower regions, the earth? ¹⁰ He who descended is the one who also ascended far above all the heavens, that he might fill all things.) ¹¹ And he gave the apostles, the prophets, the evangelists, the shepherds and teachers, ¹² to equip the saints for the work of ministry, for building up the body of Christ, ¹³ until we all attain to the unity of the faith and of the knowledge of the Son of God, to mature manhood, to the measure of the stature of the fullness of Christ, ¹⁴ so that we may no longer be children, tossed to and fro by the waves and carried about by every wind of doctrine, by human cunning, by craftiness in deceitful schemes. ¹⁵ Rather, speaking the truth in love, we are to grow up in every way into him who is the head, into Christ, ¹⁶ from whom the whole body, joined and held together by every joint with which it is equipped, when each part is working properly, makes the body grow so that it builds itself up in love.

3. REVIEW THE PAST DAY'S EVENTS (3 MINS)

- Remembering that each day is a gift from the Lord, review your day and write down a basic chronology of what happened. ☒

- Does any particular event, meeting, or place stand out to you? ☒In the rush of our days, it is easy to overlook so much. Think about the things you ate, saw, smelled and heard. Remember that God is even in these details.

4. HOW IS GOD CALLING YOU TO GREATER FAITHFULNESS (4 MINS)

- Faithfulness towards God happens in the details of our lives as much as the big decisions we make. He who is faithful with little will be faithful with much.☒

- As you consider the past day, choose one aspect that you feel God is calling you towards greater faithfulness.

- How is Christ calling you to change your motivations, your actions and your speech?

_____

_____

_____

_____

_____

_____

_____

_____

_____

_____

5. PRAY FOR THE CHANGE THAT YOU'VE IDENTIFIED (5 MINS)

- Take time to pray for insight in this one particular area of growth. Pray that God would guide you in this change towards greater faithfulness. Pray for the people involved in this matter.☒

- Praise God for His character and His promises and how He is at work in you.

- Consider the gospel and God's immense love towards you to motivate your change towards greater faithfulness.

- Remember that God patiently leads us each day. Our mistakes are redeemable and today's victories do not guarantee success tomorrow.

- Ask that you would be more aware of God's guiding presence in the day to come, and that the lessons learned today would be lived out tomorrow.

DAY 16: THE CALL FOR A NEW LIFE

1. BEGIN WITH OF AN OPENING PRAYER OF INVITATION (2 MINS)

- Sit comfortably in stillness for these minutes being reminded of God's presence.☒

- Be reminded that our God brings structure out of the chaos of our days, and leads us with His gracious hand.

- Invite the Holy Spirit who searches our hearts to guide you through this time.

2. AS YOU READ THE BIBLICAL PASSAGE, CONSIDER AND ANSWER THESE TWO QUESTIONS (8 MINS)

A. Identify one thing that this passage reveals about God?

_____

_____

_____

_____

_____

_____

_____

B. Identify one thing that this passage reveals about you/people?

_____

_____

_____

_____

_____

_____

_____

_____

Ephesians 4:17–32

The New Life

[17] Now this I say and testify in the Lord, that you must no longer walk as the Gentiles do, in the futility of their minds. [18] They are darkened in their understanding, alienated from the life of God because of the ignorance that is in them, due to their hardness of heart. [19] They have become callous and have given themselves up to sensuality, greedy to practice every kind of impurity. [20] But that is not the way you learned Christ!— [21] assuming that you have heard about him and were taught in him, as the truth is in Jesus, [22] to put off your old self, which belongs to your former manner of life and is corrupt through deceitful desires, [23] and to be renewed in the spirit of your minds, [24] and to put on the new self, created after the likeness of God in true righteousness and holiness.

[25] Therefore, having put away falsehood, let each one of you speak the truth with his neighbor, for we are members one of another. [26] Be angry and do not sin; do not let the sun go down on your anger, [27] and give no opportunity to the devil. [28] Let the thief no longer steal, but rather let him labor, doing honest work with his own hands, so that he may have something to share with anyone in need. [29] Let no corrupting talk come out of your mouths, but only such as is good for building up, as fits the occasion, that it may give grace to those who hear. [30] And do not grieve the Holy Spirit of God, by whom you were sealed for the day of redemption. [31] Let all bitterness and wrath and anger and clamor and slander be put away from you, along with all malice. [32] Be kind to one another, tenderhearted, forgiving one another, as God in Christ forgave you.

3. REVIEW THE PAST DAY'S EVENTS (3 MINS)

- Remembering that each day is a gift from the Lord, review your day and write down a basic chronology of what happened. ☒

- Does any particular event, meeting, or place stand out to you? ☒ In the rush of our days, it is easy to overlook so much. Think about the things you ate, saw, smelled and heard. Remember that God is even in these details.

_____

_____

_____

_____

_____

_____

_____

_____

_____

_____

_____

_____

_____

_____

_____

_____

_____

_____

_____

_____

_____

_____

_____

_____

_____

4. HOW IS GOD CALLING YOU TO GREATER FAITHFULNESS (4 MINS)

- Faithfulness towards God happens in the details of our lives as much as the big decisions we make. He who is faithful with little will be faithful with much.☒

- As you consider the past day, choose one aspect that you feel God is calling you towards greater faithfulness.

- How is Christ calling you to change your motivations, your actions and your speech?

_____

_____

_____

_____

_____

_____

_____

_____

_____

_____

5. PRAY FOR THE CHANGE THAT YOU'VE IDENTIFIED (5 MINS)

- Take time to pray for insight in this one particular area of growth. Pray that God would guide you in this change towards greater faithfulness. Pray for the people involved in this matter.☒

- Praise God for His character and His promises and how He is at work in you.

- Consider the gospel and God's immense love towards you to motivate your change towards greater faithfulness.

- Remember that God patiently leads us each day. Our mistakes are redeemable and today's victories do not guarantee success tomorrow.

- Ask that you would be more aware of God's guiding presence in the day to come, and that the lessons learned today would be lived out tomorrow.

DAY 17: THE CALL TO IMITATE GOD

1. BEGIN WITH OF AN OPENING PRAYER OF INVITATION (2 MINS)

- Sit comfortably in stillness for these minutes being reminded of God's presence.☒

- Be reminded that our God brings structure out of the chaos of our days, and leads us with His gracious hand.

- Invite the Holy Spirit who searches our hearts to guide you through this time.

2. AS YOU READ THE BIBLICAL PASSAGE, CONSIDER AND ANSWER THESE TWO QUESTIONS (8 MINS)

A. Identify one thing that this passage reveals about God?

_____

_____

_____

_____

_____

_____

_____

B. Identify one thing that this passage reveals about you/people?

_____

_____

_____

_____

_____

_____

_____

_____

Ephesians 5:1–21

Walk in Love

Therefore be imitators of God, as beloved children. [2] And walk in love, as Christ loved us and gave himself up for us, a fragrant offering and sacrifice to God.

[3] But sexual immorality and all impurity or covetousness must not even be named among you, as is proper among saints. [4] Let there be no filthiness nor foolish talk nor crude joking, which are out of place, but instead let there be thanksgiving. [5] For you may be sure of this, that everyone who is sexually immoral or impure, or who is covetous (that is, an idolater), has no inheritance in the kingdom of Christ and God. [6] Let no one deceive you with empty words, for because of these things the wrath of God comes upon the sons of disobedience. [7] Therefore do not become partners with them; [8] for at one time you were darkness, but now you are light in the Lord. Walk as children of light [9] (for the fruit of light is found in all that is good and right and true), [10] and try to discern what is pleasing to the Lord. [11] Take no part in the unfruitful works of darkness, but instead expose them. [12] For it is shameful even to speak of the things that they do in secret. [13] But when anything is exposed by the light, it becomes visible, [14] for anything that becomes visible is light. Therefore it says,

> "Awake, O sleeper, and arise from the dead,
> and Christ will shine on you."

[15] Look carefully then how you walk, not as unwise but as wise, [16] making the best use of the time, because the days are evil. [17] Therefore do not be foolish, but understand what the will of the Lord is. [18] And do not get drunk with wine, for that is debauchery, but be filled with the Spirit, [19] addressing one another in psalms and hymns and spiritual songs, singing and making melody to the Lord with your heart, [20] giving thanks always and for everything to God the Father in the name of our Lord Jesus Christ, [21] submitting to one another out of reverence for Christ.

3. REVIEW THE PAST DAY'S EVENTS (3 MINS)

- Remembering that each day is a gift from the Lord, review your day and write down a basic chronology of what happened. ☒

- Does any particular event, meeting, or place stand out to you? ☒In the rush of our days, it is easy to overlook so much. Think about the things you ate, saw, smelled and heard. Remember that God is even in these details.

_____

_____

_____

_____

_____

_____

_____

_____

_____

_____

_____

_____

_____

_____

_____

_____

_____

_____

_____

_____

_____

_____

_____

_____

4. HOW IS GOD CALLING YOU TO GREATER FAITHFULNESS (4 MINS)

- Faithfulness towards God happens in the details of our lives as much as the big decisions we make. He who is faithful with little will be faithful with much.☒

- As you consider the past day, choose one aspect that you feel God is calling you towards greater faithfulness.

- How is Christ calling you to change your motivations, your actions and your speech?

_____

_____

_____

_____

_____

_____

_____

_____

_____

_____

5. PRAY FOR THE CHANGE THAT YOU'VE IDENTIFIED (5 MINS)

- Take time to pray for insight in this one particular area of growth. Pray that God would guide you in this change towards greater faithfulness. Pray for the people involved in this matter.☒

- Praise God for His character and His promises and how He is at work in you.

- Consider the gospel and God's immense love towards you to motivate your change towards greater faithfulness.

- Remember that God patiently leads us each day. Our mistakes are redeemable and today's victories do not guarantee success tomorrow.

- Ask that you would be more aware of God's guiding presence in the day to come, and that the lessons learned today would be lived out tomorrow.

DAY 18: THE CALL TO HOLINESS

1. BEGIN WITH OF AN OPENING PRAYER OF INVITATION (2 MINS)

- Sit comfortably in stillness for these minutes being reminded of God's presence.☒

- Be reminded that our God brings structure out of the chaos of our days, and leads us with His gracious hand.

- Invite the Holy Spirit who searches our hearts to guide you through this time.

2. AS YOU READ THE BIBLICAL PASSAGE, CONSIDER AND ANSWER THESE TWO QUESTIONS (8 MINS)

A. Identify one thing that this passage reveals about God?

_____

_____

_____

_____

_____

_____

_____

B. Identify one thing that this passage reveals about you/people?

_____

_____

_____

_____

_____

_____

_____

1 Peter 2:1-12

A Living Stone and a Holy People

So put away all malice and all deceit and hypocrisy and envy and all slander. [2] Like newborn infants, long for the pure spiritual milk, that by it you may grow up into salvation— [3] if indeed you have tasted that the Lord is good.

[4] As you come to him, a living stone rejected by men but in the sight of God chosen and precious, [5] you yourselves like living stones are being built up as a spiritual house, to be a holy priesthood, to offer spiritual sacrifices acceptable to God through Jesus Christ. [6] For it stands in Scripture:

"Behold, I am laying in Zion a stone, a cornerstone chosen and precious, and whoever believes in him will not be put to shame."

[7] So the honor is for you who believe, but for those who do not believe,

"The stone that the builders rejected has become the cornerstone,"

[8] and "A stone of stumbling and a rock of offense."

They stumble because they disobey the word, as they were destined to do.

[9] But you are a chosen race, a royal priesthood, a holy nation, a people for his own possession, that you may proclaim the excellencies of him who called you out of darkness into his marvelous light. [10] Once you were not a people, but now you are God's people; once you had not received mercy, but now you have received mercy.

[11] Beloved, I urge you as sojourners and exiles to abstain from the passions of the flesh, which wage war against your soul. [12] Keep your conduct among the Gentiles honorable, so that when they speak against you as evildoers, they may see your good deeds and glorify God on the day of visitation.

3. REVIEW THE PAST DAY'S EVENTS (3 MINS)

- Remembering that each day is a gift from the Lord, review your day and write down a basic chronology of what happened. ☒

- Does any particular event, meeting, or place stand out to you? ☒ In the rush of our days, it is easy to overlook so much. Think about the things you ate, saw, smelled and heard. Remember that God is even in these details.

4. HOW IS GOD CALLING YOU TO GREATER FAITHFULNESS (4 MINS)

- Faithfulness towards God happens in the details of our lives as much as the big decisions we make. He who is faithful with little will be faithful with much. ☒

- As you consider the past day, choose one aspect that you feel God is calling you towards greater faithfulness.

- How is Christ calling you to change your motivations, your actions and your speech?

_____

_____

_____

_____

_____

_____

_____

_____

_____

5. PRAY FOR THE CHANGE THAT YOU'VE IDENTIFIED (5 MINS)

- Take time to pray for insight in this one particular area of growth. Pray that God would guide you in this change towards greater faithfulness. Pray for the people involved in this matter. ☒

- Praise God for His character and His promises and how He is at work in you.

- Consider the gospel and God's immense love towards you to motivate your change towards greater faithfulness.

- Remember that God patiently leads us each day. Our mistakes are redeemable and today's victories do not guarantee success tomorrow.

- Ask that you would be more aware of God's guiding presence in the day to come, and that the lessons learned today would be lived out tomorrow.

DAY 19: THE CALL TO FAITHFULNESS

1. BEGIN WITH OF AN OPENING PRAYER OF INVITATION (2 MINS)

- Sit comfortably in stillness for these minutes being reminded of God's presence.☒

- Be reminded that our God brings structure out of the chaos of our days, and leads us with His gracious hand.

- Invite the Holy Spirit who searches our hearts to guide you through this time.

2. AS YOU READ THE BIBLICAL PASSAGE, CONSIDER AND ANSWER THESE TWO QUESTIONS (8 MINS)

A. Identify one thing that this passage reveals about God?

_____

_____

_____

_____

_____

_____

_____

B. Identify one thing that this passage reveals about you/people?

_____

_____

_____

_____

_____

_____

_____

_____

Hebrews 3:5-19

⁵ Now Moses was faithful in all God's house as a servant, to testify to the things that were to be spoken later, ⁶ but Christ is faithful over God's house as a son. And we are his house if indeed we hold fast our confidence and our boasting in our hope.

7 Therefore, as the Holy Spirit says, "Today, if you hear his voice,
    8   do not harden your hearts as in the rebellion,
          on the day of testing in the wilderness,
    9   where your fathers put me to the test
          and saw my works for forty years.
    10   Therefore I was provoked with that generation,
          and said, 'They always go astray in their heart;
          they have not known my ways.'
    11   As I swore in my wrath, 'They shall not enter my rest.' "

¹² Take care, brothers, lest there be in any of you an evil, unbelieving heart, leading you to fall away from the living God. ¹³ But exhort one another every day, as long as it is called "today," that none of you may be hardened by the deceitfulness of sin. ¹⁴ For we have come to share in Christ, if indeed we hold our original confidence firm to the end. ¹⁵ As it is said,

> "Today, if you hear his voice,
> do not harden your hearts as in the rebellion."

¹⁶ For who were those who heard and yet rebelled? Was it not all those who left Egypt led by Moses? ¹⁷ And with whom was he provoked for forty years? Was it not with those who sinned, whose bodies fell in the wilderness? ¹⁸ And to whom did he swear that they would not enter his rest, but to those who were disobedient? ¹⁹ So we see that they were unable to enter because of unbelief.

3. REVIEW THE PAST DAY'S EVENTS (3 MINS)

- Remembering that each day is a gift from the Lord, review your day and write down a basic chronology of what happened. ☒

- Does any particular event, meeting, or place stand out to you? ☒In the rush of our days, it is easy to overlook so much. Think about the things you ate, saw, smelled and heard. Remember that God is even in these details.

4. HOW IS GOD CALLING YOU TO GREATER FAITHFULNESS (4 MINS)

- Faithfulness towards God happens in the details of our lives as much as the big decisions we make. He who is faithful with little will be faithful with much.☒

- As you consider the past day, choose one aspect that you feel God is calling you towards greater faithfulness.

- How is Christ calling you to change your motivations, your actions and your speech?

_____

_____

_____

_____

_____

_____

_____

_____

_____

5. PRAY FOR THE CHANGE THAT YOU'VE IDENTIFIED (5 MINS)

- Take time to pray for insight in this one particular area of growth. Pray that God would guide you in this change towards greater faithfulness. Pray for the people involved in this matter.☒

- Praise God for His character and His promises and how He is at work in you.

- Consider the gospel and God's immense love towards you to motivate your change towards greater faithfulness.

- Remember that God patiently leads us each day. Our mistakes are redeemable and today's victories do not guarantee success tomorrow.

- Ask that you would be more aware of God's guiding presence in the day to come, and that the lessons learned today would be lived out tomorrow.

DAY 20: THE CALL TO WORSHIP

1. BEGIN WITH OF AN OPENING PRAYER OF INVITATION (2 MINS)

- Sit comfortably in stillness for these minutes being reminded of God's presence. ☒

- Be reminded that our God brings structure out of the chaos of our days, and leads us with His gracious hand.

- Invite the Holy Spirit who searches our hearts to guide you through this time.

2. AS YOU READ THE BIBLICAL PASSAGE, CONSIDER AND ANSWER THESE TWO QUESTIONS (8 MINS)

A. Identify one thing that this passage reveals about God?

_____

_____

_____

_____

_____

_____

B. Identify one thing that this passage reveals about you/people?

_____

_____

_____

_____

_____

_____

_____

Psalm 19

The Law of the LORD Is Perfect

To the choirmaster. A Psalm of David.

1   The heavens declare the glory of God,
and the sky above proclaims his handiwork.

2   Day to day pours out speech,
and night to night reveals knowledge.

3   There is no speech, nor are there words,
whose voice is not heard.

4   Their voice goes out through all the earth,
and their words to the end of the world.

      In them he has set a tent for the sun,

5   which comes out like a bridegroom leaving his chamber,
and, like a strong man, runs its course with joy.

6   Its rising is from the end of the heavens,
and its circuit to the end of them,
and there is nothing hidden from its heat.

7   The law of the Lord is perfect,
reviving the soul;

      the testimony of the Lord is sure,
making wise the simple;

8   the precepts of the Lord are right,
rejoicing the heart;

      the commandment of the Lord is pure,
enlightening the eyes;

9   the fear of the Lord is clean,
enduring forever;

      the rules of the Lord are true,
and righteous altogether.

10   More to be desired are they than gold,
even much fine gold;

      sweeter also than honey
and drippings of the honeycomb.

11   Moreover, by them is your servant warned;
in keeping them there is great reward.

12   Who can discern his errors?
Declare me innocent from hidden faults.

13   Keep back your servant also from presumptuous sins;
let them not have dominion over me!

      Then I shall be blameless,
and innocent of great transgression.

14   Let the words of my mouth and the meditation of my heart
be acceptable in your sight, O Lord, my rock and my redeemer.

3. REVIEW THE PAST DAY'S EVENTS (3 MINS)

- Remembering that each day is a gift from the Lord, review your day and write down a basic chronology of what happened. ☒

- Does any particular event, meeting, or place stand out to you? ☒ In the rush of our days, it is easy to overlook so much. Think about the things you ate, saw, smelled and heard. Remember that God is even in these details.

_____

_____

_____

_____

_____

_____

_____

_____

_____

_____

_____

_____

_____

_____

_____

_____

_____

_____

_____

_____

_____

_____

_____

_____

_____

4. HOW IS GOD CALLING YOU TO GREATER FAITHFULNESS (4 MINS)

- Faithfulness towards God happens in the details of our lives as much as the big decisions we make. He who is faithful with little will be faithful with much.☒

- As you consider the past day, choose one aspect that you feel God is calling you towards greater faithfulness.

- How is Christ calling you to change your motivations, your actions and your speech?

_____

_____

_____

_____

_____

_____

_____

_____

_____

_____

5. PRAY FOR THE CHANGE THAT YOU'VE IDENTIFIED (5 MINS)

- Take time to pray for insight in this one particular area of growth. Pray that God would guide you in this change towards greater faithfulness. Pray for the people involved in this matter.☒

- Praise God for His character and His promises and how He is at work in you.

- Consider the gospel and God's immense love towards you to motivate your change towards greater faithfulness.

- Remember that God patiently leads us each day. Our mistakes are redeemable and today's victories do not guarantee success tomorrow.

- Ask that you would be more aware of God's guiding presence in the day to come, and that the lessons learned today would be lived out tomorrow.

ABOUT THE AUTHOR

David H. Kim is the Executive Director of the Center for Faith & Work (CFW) and Pastor of Faith & Work at Redeemer Presbyterian Church in Manhattan and also serves on Redeemer's Executive Team. David joined the CFW team in 2007 to create, develop, and implement the Gotham Fellowship, an intensive leadership development program for professionals that serves to bridge theology & application in professional contexts. Prior to joining CFW, David served as a Chaplain at Princeton University as well as Founding Director of Manna Christian Fellowship for over twelve years.

He received his B.A. from the University of Pennsylvania, his M.Div. from Westminster Theological Seminary, and his Th.M. from Princeton Theological Seminary. Currently, he is finishing his D.Min. at Fuller Theological Seminary. David was a founding editor of *Revisions*, a Journal of Christian perspective at Princeton University. He has written *TWENTY AND SOMETHING: Have the Time of Your Life (Without Wasting Any of It)* and two devotional book, *Glimpses of a Greater Glory: A Devotional through the Storyline of the Bible* and *The Lord's Prayer Devotional*. He is the general editor of a forthcoming Faith and Work Bible (published by Zondervan in fall 2016).

Made in the USA
Lexington, KY
06 February 2018